FIRST NATIONS OF NORTH AMERICA

CALIFORNIA INDIANS

LIZ SONNEBORN

HEINEMANN LIBRARY
CHICAGO, ILLINOIS

www.heinemannraintree.com
Visit our website to find out
more information about
Heinemann-Raintree books.

To order:

☎ Phone 888-454-2279

🖥 Visit www.heinemannraintree.com
to browse our catalog and order online.

Original illustrations © Capstone Global Library, Ltd.
Illustrated by Mapping Specialists, Ltd.
Originated by Capstone Global Library, Ltd.
Printed in China by China Translation and Printing Services

14 13 12 11
10 9 8 7 6 5 4 3 2 1

Library of Congress Cataloging-in-Publication Data
Sonneborn, Liz.
  California Indians / Liz Sonneborn.
    p. cm.—(First Nations of North America)
  Includes bibliographical references and index.
  ISBN 978-1-4329-4946-4 (hc)—
ISBN 978-1-4329-4957-0 (pb) 1. Indians of North America—
California—Juvenile literature. I. Title.
  E78.C15S683 2012
  978.004'97—dc22   2010040611

Acknowledgments
The author and publisher are grateful to the following for
permission to reproduce copyright material: Alamy: p. 41
(© Peter Horree); Corbis: pp. 22 (© Corbis), 31 (© National
Geographic Society), 37 (© Bettmann); Library of Congress
Prints and Photographs Division: pp. 5, 8, 13, 15, 18, 25, 36;
National Geographic Stock: pp. 12 (W. LANGDON KIHN), 24
(PHIL SCHERMEISTER), 33 (ROBERT SISSON); Nativestock.
com: pp. 4 (© Marilyn Angel Wynn), 14 (© Marilyn Angel
Wynn), 17 (© Marilyn Angel Wynn), 19 (© Marilyn Angel
Wynn), 21 (© Marilyn Angel Wynn), 23 (© Marilyn Angel
Wynn), 30 (© Marilyn Angel Wynn), 39 (© Marilyn Angel
Wynn), 40 (© Marilyn Angel Wynn); Photolibrary: p. 27
(Nativestock Pictures); Shutterstock: pp. 10 (© Andy Z.), 29
(© Andy Z.); The Granger Collection: pp. 26, 32, 24.

Cover photograph of a Pomo gift basket reproduced with
permission from The Bridgeman Art Library International (©
Boltin Picture Library).

We would like to thank Dr. Scott Stevens for his invaluable
help in the preparation of this book.

Every effort has been made to contact copyright holders of
any material reproduced in this book. Any omissions will
be rectified in subsequent printings if notice is given to
the publisher.

All the Internet addresses (URLs) given in this book were valid
at the time of going to press. However, due to the dynamic
nature of the Internet, some addresses may have changed, or
sites may have changed or ceased to exist since publication.
While the author and publisher regret any inconvenience this
may cause readers, no responsibility for any such changes can
be accepted by either the author or the publisher.

Contents

Some words are shown in bold **like this**. You can find out what they mean by looking in the glossary.

Who Were the First People in North America?

According to legend, Hutash was the Earth Goddess. On an island, she made the first people from the seeds of a magic plant. Her husband was Sky Snake. From his tongue, he aimed a lightning bolt at the people. It gave the humans the gift of fire.

Soon, their population grew. The island could barely hold all the people. Hutash became annoyed by all the noise they made. She decided they needed to move to the mainland. Hutash then created a bridge from a rainbow. As the people walked along the rainbow bridge, some tumbled into the water below. They turned into dolphins. But most of Hutash's people arrived safely in their new home. They have lived there ever since.

▶ The **ancestors** of this American Indian child probably first arrived in California about 10,000 years ago.

◄ Photographed in 1924, this Yokut man stands in a pool of water in central California, where his people had lived for thousands of years.

This is a story told by the Chumash to explain how they came to their **homeland** in present-day California. The Chumash are Native Americans, also called American Indians. Today's American Indians are the **descendants** of the first people to live in North America and South America.

American Indian or Native American?

The original people of the Americas are often called American Indians. The term comes from a mistake made by explorer Christopher Columbus. When he first arrived in North America in 1492, he thought he was in India. Columbus naturally called the people he met Indians.

Today, some **native** peoples in the United States still call themselves American Indians. But others prefer to call themselves Native Americans. Many prefer to be called by their tribal **affiliation**, such as Chumash.

From Asia to America

Scientists believe the first people came to North America from Asia. They probably arrived more than 12,000 years ago.

Back then, Earth's temperature was much colder. The Bering Strait, the waterway that now separates North America and Asia, was frozen over. A strip of land beneath the Bering Strait was exposed.

People from Asia began walking across this land bridge. They were probably hunters who were following large **game** animals. These humans and their descendants continued moving south.

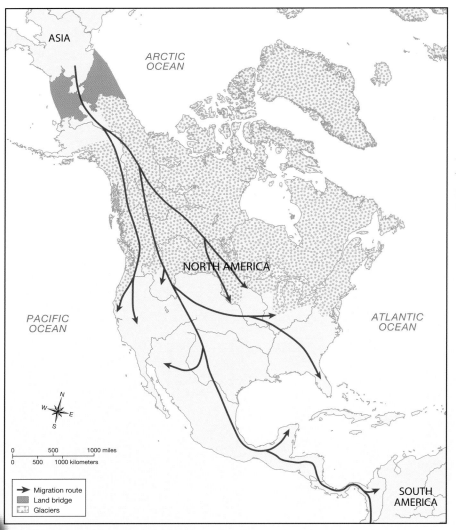

◄ This map shows the routes of the first people who came to North America.

◄ This map shows the different regions of the first people of North America.

Over a long period of time, people settled in regions all over North America and South America. About 10,000 years ago, early American Indians were probably living in the California **culture area**.

500 tribes

Non-Indians came to North America beginning in 1492. At that time, about 500 Indian **tribes** lived in what became the United States. Each of these tribes had its own ways of life and its own beliefs.

Experts who study how people lived long ago are called **anthropologists**. They have found that tribes in certain regions shared similar ways of life. Anthropologists call these regions culture areas.

Who Are California Indians?

The California **culture area** is located mostly within the borders of the modern state of California. Today, about 330,000 American Indians live in this area.

A land of plenty

Before non-Indians arrived, the California culture area was home to about 100 **tribes**. Most of these tribes had fairly small populations. Often, they were made up of only a few hundred people.

▲ Traveling in canoes, early California Indians traded goods such as acorns, dried fish, and salt.

The lands of California Indians were rich in **natural resources**. Even small groups had little trouble getting the food they needed from their immediate surroundings. As a result, most early California Indians did not travel far from their homes. Many lived their entire lives without meeting anyone outside their villages.

Trading

Some traders, however, did travel long distances. Most were members of tribes that lived on the coast of the Pacific Ocean. These traders built canoes that could sail the rough ocean waters. Using these boats, they could easily visit many different coastal villages.

LANGUAGE

California Indian Place-Names

Today, names of places all over California are based on American Indian words. Here are just a few:

Hueneme Port	Quanai Canyon	Yosemite Valley
Based on a Chumash word meaning "sleeping place"	Based on a Diegueño word meaning "wire grass"	Based on a Miwok word meaning "they are killers"
Chumash traders often spent the night at this spot while traveling from village to village.	The Diegueño visited the canyon to harvest a wild grass they used to make baskets.	The Miwok considered the **native** peoples of the valley to be dangerous enemies.

In the South

Most early California Indians lived in a comfortable environment. But their **homelands** varied a good deal from place to place.

In the Southeast, coastal tribes, such as the Chumash, enjoyed beautiful beaches and cool ocean breezes. Farther inland, the climate was much hotter and drier. The territories of the Diegueño and the Cahuilla, for instance, were largely desert lands. Here and there, however, were **oases**. These were small areas watered by natural **springs**.

▲ The Chumash **traditionally** lived along the coast of the Pacific Ocean. They were once one of the largest tribes in the California culture area.

Central and northern California

Much of central California is covered by **marshes**, low-lying areas that are often flooded. Tribes such as the Pomo and the Yokut lived in these wetlands. To the east of these groups was the Sierra Nevada. The forested foothills of these mountains were home to the Miwok and the Yana. To the northwest was a rainy region thick with vegetation. The Hupa and Yurok lived in this lush rain forest.

Early California Indians had a similar way of life, though their ways varied slightly depending on their environment. But no matter where they lived, California Indians took full advantage of the many resources their lands offered.

▲ This map shows where many tribes of the California culture area lived.

What Did Early California Indians Eat?

In most regions of North America, early Indians grew at least some of their food. But in California, few Indians farmed. Their lands were so full of wild plants and animals that they did not need to grow their own food.

▲ Every autumn, the Pomo Indians worked together to collect ripe acorns during the **annual** harvest.

Acorns

Throughout much of California, the most important food was the acorn. Acorns are the nuts of oak trees. Especially in central California, Indians had access to large forests of oaks. Each fall, when the acorns were ripe, families spent weeks collecting the nuts. They carefully stored the annual harvest so they could eat acorns year-round.

The meat of the acorn tastes bitter. California Indian women developed a way to make it more flavorful. They ground it into a meal and then poured water over it. With enough washing, the meal lost its bitterness.

Women used the meal to bake bread. They also mixed it with water to make a thick soup. People often mixed in berries to make their acorn soup even more delicious. California Indians continue the **tradition** of cooking with acorns today.

Insects for dinner

There were fewer wild foods available in the southern deserts than in other areas of California. But the Indians there did have plenty of insects to eat. One snack was grasshoppers roasted over a fire. Boiled caterpillars seasoned with salt were another.

▲ Aside from acorns, early California Indians ate many other types of wild plant foods. These included bulbs, roots, berries, seeds, and cactus leaves. This woman is using a woven seed beater to knock seeds into a basket.

13

Hunting

Early California Indians also feasted on many types of wild animals. Using bows and arrows, hunters killed large **game**, such as deer, sheep, antelope, and elk. They also hunted rabbits, squirrels, and other small animals. In **marshy** areas, ducks, geese, and swans were an important source of food.

Fishing

Along lakes and rivers, California fishermen caught a wide variety of fish, including trout, perch, and whitefish. In the Northwest, the most important fish was the salmon. Fishermen there could catch large numbers of salmon each spring, when the fish swam upstream to lay their eggs.

Fishermen used many types of fishing tools, including spears and nets. Some groups, such as the Pomo, held baskets in the water to capture fish swimming by. Others made wooden **weirs** in waterways. Weirs are fence-like fishing traps. As fish clustered inside a weir, fishermen could easily spear them.

▲ California Indian men used bows and arrows not only for hunting, but also for battling their enemies.

▲ Many of California's waterways were so full of fish that Indian fishermen could get a good catch simply by scooping a net through the water.

Food from the ocean

Early California Indians living along the Pacific Coast fished in the ocean. They hunted large sea animals, too. These included seals and sea otters. The diet of coastal Indians was also rich in shellfish. Walking along the beach, they collected **mussels**, clams, oysters, and **scallops**. If a coastal **tribe** was lucky, a whale would wash up on shore. An entire village could then enjoy a hearty meal of whale meat.

What Were Early California Indian Houses Like?

Early California Indians built many different types of houses. The kind of house they had depended on where they lived.

Shelter from the cold and rain

In the Northwest, California Indians built very sturdy houses. These were made from wooden planks. Plank houses shielded people from the heavy rainstorms that were common in the region.

In cool areas, people spent the winter in pit houses. Their floors were deep pits dug into the ground. The pits were topped by wooden frames covered with dirt. A pit house was warm even when it was very cold outside.

Warm weather dwellings

A popular type of house in central California started with a simple dome-shaped frame. House builders made the frame from saplings—the bendable trunks of small trees. Over the frame, they tied on mats to form walls. The mats were woven from grasses or **reeds**.

In the Sierra Nevada foothills, California Indians built small cone-shaped dwellings. These were covered with bark, a material widely available in nearby forests.

In the southern desert, California Indians built very simple brush shelters with **ramadas.** Sitting under these raised platforms, families were shaded from the hot Sun.

Sweathouses

Many villages also included a **sweathouse**. In the middle of a sweathouse was a fire pit. Men sitting around the fire began to sweat heavily. They believed that spending time in a sweathouse **purified** their bodies and kept them healthy.

▲ In central California, many people covered their houses with mats made of **tule**. Tule is a plant that grows wild in **marshy** areas.

◄ In northwest California, Indians wore hats that were woven like baskets. They were waterproof enough to wear in the rain.

Clothing

Because of the pleasant weather in their lands, many early California Indians needed little clothing. In especially warm areas, men and children usually wore nothing. Women wore fringed aprons. These were made of leather or woven from grass or bark. Generally, people wore sandals or went barefoot.

To the north, when the weather was cool, California Indians wore shoes similar to **moccasins** on their feet. Moccasins are soft leather shoes that looked a little like slippers. People also wrapped themselves in robes made of animal furs. Rabbit-skin robes were especially popular. People living along the coast liked robes made of sea otter skins. These robes were both warm and waterproof.

Jewelry

Early California Indians enjoyed wearing jewelry. They made necklaces, earrings, and ornaments for their hair. They crafted their jewelry out of shells, stones, bones, and feathers. Sometimes, people decorated their bodies with paints made from plants. In the North, they also used plant dyes to tattoo themselves.

Dressing in feathers

Eagles and condors soared high above the lands of the California Indians. The Indians used the feathers of these great birds to make robes and headdresses. Important leaders wore these feathered garments during religious **ceremonies** and other special events.

▲ These Indian men from southern California are wearing **traditional** feathered headdresses and face and body paint.

What Was Everyday Life Like for Early California Indians?

For early California Indians, what someone did every day depended on whether the person was a woman or a man.

Women cooked for their families. They also gathered wild plant foods, such as berries and roots. Another important job of women was making baskets.

Men also had to work, but at different tasks. They fished and hunted to provide food for their relatives. They also made all the tools they needed to hunt and fish.

Educating children

Adults were expected to educate their children. Parents showed their children how to perform the jobs they would do when they grew up.

Children also learned from their grandparents. Grandparents told their grandchildren old stories. Children loved hearing these tales. The stories were not just entertaining, though. They taught children valuable lessons about how to behave.

A Day in the Life of an Early California Indian Boy

Usually, the daily life of an early California Indian boy was full of play. Once he was a teenager, he would have to join his father on hunting and fishing **expeditions**. But as a boy, he usually did not have to work. He might, however, use a toy bow and arrow to hunt small animals, such as squirrels and frogs. He might also spend time swimming or playing ball games with his friends. In the evening, a boy might sit quietly while listening to a grandparent tell one of his **tribe's** old stories.

▲ Throughout California, **elders** shared traditional stories with the children of their tribe.

Maintaining order

Early California Indians had a strict code of behavior. They were always supposed to put the good of the group above their own desires. Even so, disagreements between people and families did sometimes happen. These problems were usually settled by village leaders. Often, a leader had a council of elders to advise him. Leaders made a variety of decisions, such as where to go on hunting expeditions or when to perform **ceremonies**. Sometimes, they decided to go to war with other communities, but only rarely. Leaders always tried to settle problems peacefully before **resorting** to violence.

Celebrating the harvest

Generally, early California Indians had little contact with people outside their village. Fall provided one exception. Then, during the **annual** fall acorn harvest, large groups of people came together in oak forests to collect ripened acorns. For weeks, they worked hard to harvest as many nuts as they could. But the harvest was also a time to play. During the harvest season, people enjoyed feasting, dancing, **gambling**, and visiting with one another.

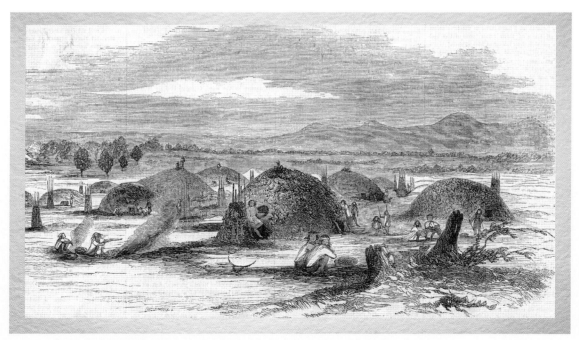

▲ This picture shows an Indian village in central California in the mid-1800s.

Playing sports

At social gatherings, early California Indians also liked to play sports. They often held wrestling contests and footraces, with those watching betting on who would win. They also fielded teams to play a game similar to the modern-day sport of **lacrosse**. Both men and women played, but never against each other.

▲ Many children enjoyed playing the pole and hoop game. Players tried to throw a pole through the center of a rolling hoop made of willow bark.

What Objects Did Early California Indians Make?

Early California Indian women were expert basket makers. They created baskets by weaving grasses, **tule**, and other plants. Many modern California Indians continue this **tradition** today.

Making baskets

Some of the California Indians' baskets were decorated with colorful designs. To create these designs, basket makers dyed their weaving materials different colors. They made the dyes from flowers and berries.

▲ A skilled basket weaver could make baskets of different sizes and shapes. California Indians carry on the tradition of basket making today.

Mabel McKay

A member of the Pomo **tribe**, Mabel McKay (1907–1993) was one of the most famous California Indian basket makers. Since she was as a little girl, she had visions of spirits. She believed the spirits helped her cure sick people. She said they also taught her how to weave baskets. Throughout her life, she shared her knowledge of Pomo ways, including basket making, with others. Her baskets can be found in museums across the United States.

Uses for baskets

The baskets of early California Indians had many uses. Some baskets held the wild plants they gathered. Others stored important foods such as acorn meal. Women used very tightly woven baskets to boil water for cooking. Basket weavers also made hats for people to shield themselves from the Sun and mats to cover their houses.

Some tribes made baskets that had no practical use. They were just meant to be beautiful objects. The Pomo, for instance, are still well-known for their artistic baskets. Pomo weavers often decorate their works with feathers and beads. To show off their skills, they also make miniature baskets—some as small as a thumbnail.

▲ Women often placed their youngest children in woven baby carriers as they went about their chores.

25

Tools

In addition to baskets, early California Indians crafted a wide variety of tools to help them perform their daily work. Some tools were very simple. For example, women used a stick sharpened on one end to poke roots out of the ground.

Other tools were more difficult to make and use. These included the many tools made by hunters and fishermen. They chipped stone to make spear points and arrowheads. They wove plant materials to create fishing nets. And they used wood to construct **weirs**. Craftspeople also used wood, shells, and animal horns to make everyday things such as bowls and spoons.

Boat making

Some early California Indians were skilled at making boats, which they used for fishing trips and trading **expeditions**. The Pomo made rafts by lashing together tule rushes. These vessels, however, easily absorbed water. They often had to be carried to shore where they could dry out in the Sun. The Yurok made much more seaworthy canoes by digging out the center of logs from redwood trees.

◄ Coastal California Indians carved simple sculptures of animals out of a soft black stone. They carried them for luck on hunting and fishing trips.

The Chumash's boats, called **tomols**, were perhaps the most impressive of all. *Tomols* measured up to 30 feet (9 meters) long. They were made of planks of wood stitched with leather or plant materials. A coating of natural tar also helped hold the planks together.

▲ California Indian traders used strings of shell beads for money.

What Did Early California Indians Believe?

Early California Indians believed that there were spiritual forces in all natural things. To honor these spirits, they prayed while going about their daily tasks. Basket makers sang special songs to the spirits while they collected the grasses they would weave. Fishermen offered thanks to the fish that gave up their lives to feed the fishermen's families.

How Coyote Became Clever

Coyote was a favorite character in many **traditional** stories of California Indians. In one Coyote tale, told by the Karok **tribe**, the Creator instructed the first man to make a bow for every animal on Earth. The longer an animal's bow, the more powerful the animal would be.

Coyote wanted the longest bow. He tried to stay up all night, so he would be first in line. But come morning, he fell asleep. When he woke up, the man had handed out all the bows but one—the very shortest. The other animals laughed at Coyote, because he would be the weakest of all of them. The man felt sorry for Coyote and prayed to the Creator. The Creator responded by giving Coyote the gift of a clever mind.

Stories of the spirit world

Early California Indians also told stories about the spirits. These stories explain how the world had come to be. The Shasta, for instance, told of a spirit who cut a hole in the sky. He then pushed snow and ice through it. As the snow fell to the Earth, it created the mighty Mount Shasta.

▲ Mount Shasta is still considered a sacred site by many Indians in northern California.

Spiritual leaders

California Indians wanted to keep the spirits happy. If they did not, they feared the spirits would punish them with a flood, an earthquake, or another natural disaster. To keep the world in balance, the Indians performed **ceremonies**. Some tribes continue to perform their traditional ceremonies today.

Spiritual leaders oversaw the ceremonies. They were thought to have special powers that they received in dreams or visions.

Ceremonies

Tribes performed ceremonies for many reasons. A ceremony might honor people who died, or it might offer thanks to the spirits. Some ceremonies marked a boy's or a girl's passage from childhood to adulthood.

▲ A family of Pomo Indians dances wearing traditional ceremonial clothing during the Indian Days Festival in Novato, California. California Indians today carry on many of the traditional ceremonies of their ancestors.

Generally, people participating in ceremonies wore special clothing, such as feathered headdresses and aprons decorated with animal skins. They also usually danced and sang songs. California Indians still make a wide variety of instruments to create ceremonial music. These include drums, whistles, and rattles made from turtle shells or deer hooves.

Some ceremonies were very elaborate. For instance, every fall the Hupa and other northwestern groups devoted 10 days to the White Deerskin Dance. Dancers wore deerskins on their backs while imitating the movements of deer. Only men could dance, but women prepared the feasts that were part of the ceremony. By performing the White Deerskin Dance, the Hupa believed they were renewing the world and ensuring their good fortune in the year ahead. Many of these celebrations are still practiced today.

▲ During the White Deerskin Dance, Hupa dancers carried high poles on which they draped the skins of deer.

When Did California Indians Meet Non-Indians?

For thousands of years, California Indians had little contact with anyone else—either Indian or non-Indian.

Meeting Spaniards

In 1543, however, a group of non-Indians from Spain came to present-day California. Led by Portuguese explorer Juan Rodríguez Cabrillo, they sailed up most of the California coastline. When Indians along the coast saw the Spaniards' great ships, they paddled out in canoes to greet the strangers.

▲ Indians of California's northern coast encountered Englishmen led by Sir Francis Drake in 1579.

The English arrive

Thirty-six years later, another **expedition** of non-Indians arrived on the northern California Coast. This expedition included English explorers led by Sir Francis Drake. Again, Indians welcomed these newcomers and offered them gifts.

Even though these encounters were friendly, few non-Indians came to California after these expeditions. In fact, more than 150 years would pass before California Indians had much contact with non-Indians again.

BIOGRAPHY

Juana Maria

For centuries, a branch of Chumash Indians lived on San Nicolas, an island off the coast of what is now Los Angeles, California. In the 1830s, the Mexican government decided to move the Indians to the mainland. However, a young woman named Juana Maria (unknown–1853) was left behind. For 18 years, she lived alone on the island. Like the rest of her people, she died of a disease soon after she was found by a group of non-Indian hunters. Her story inspired the classic young adult novel *Island of the Blue Dolphins* by Scott O'Dell.

▲ Sea lions gather on the beach of San Nicolas Island, which was once the **homeland** of one branch of the Chumash Indians.

How Did Life Change After Meeting Non-Indians?

In the 1760s, the government of Spain decided to try to take control of southern California. It sent soldiers to build settlements there. It also sent Catholic priests. They were supposed to **convert** the Indians to the religion of Christianity.

Non-Indian diseases

These Spaniards brought something deadly to California—diseases such as **measles** and **smallpox**. California Indians had never been exposed to these diseases before. Their bodies had not developed any protection against them. As a result, when Indians caught the diseases, they usually died. Some villages lost as many as nine out of every ten people.

▲ At Spanish missions, California Indians had to work long hours. If they did not obey the Spaniards there, they could expect harsh punishment.

Spanish missions

Many of the survivors of those diseases went to live near **missions**. These were buildings constructed by the Spanish. At missions, Spanish priests fed the Indians, many of whom were starving. But the priests also forced them to work. In addition, the Spanish made the Indians give up their religion and become Christians. If Indians resisted, the Spanish beat them.

However, Indians often fought back. In 1785 a young Gabrielino Indian woman named Toypurina led an attack on the San Gabriel mission. The attack did not succeed. The Spanish caught her and sent her away from the land of her people.

The mission system came to an end in the 1830s. Mission Indians were then free to leave and return to their old way of life.

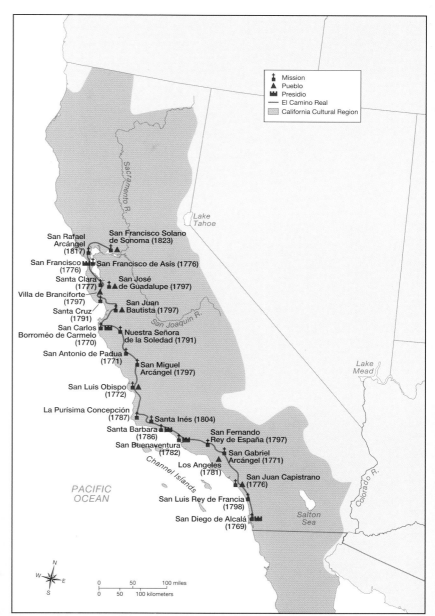

▲ This map shows all of the Spanish missions in the California Indian cultural area.

Americans move west to California

In the 1800s, people from what is now the eastern United States came to California. At first, they were mostly farmers, attracted by its rich farmland.

In 1848 gold was discovered in California. Soon people from all over the world flocked there. The **California Gold Rush** was a terrible time for California Indians. Many died of non-Indian diseases. Others were murdered by **miners** who wanted their land. Still others died of hunger when they lost control of their hunting and fishing sites.

Reservations

California became a state in 1850. Its government forced many of the surviving Indians onto small areas of land called **reservations**. Americans then took over the Indians' old territories.

▲ In the late 1800s, many California Indians were forced onto reservations, like the one pictured above.

Moving to California's cities

In the 1950s and 1960s, the U.S. government encouraged Indians from other parts of the country to move to California. They settled in large cities, such as San Francisco and Los Angeles. There, Indians of various **tribes** came together in the 1970s to protest against government policies they thought were unfair.

BIOGRAPHY

Hurting the Earth's Spirit

American miners destroyed much of the California countryside. A Wintu Indian woman named Kate Luckie later described the damage: "The white people never cared for land or deer or bear.... [They] plow up the ground, pull down the trees, kill everything.... How can the spirit of the earth like the White man?... Everywhere the White man has touched it, it is sore."

▲ Leaders of the American Indian Movement hold a press conference at Alcatraz Federal Penitentiary during their takeover between 1969 and 1970.

How Do California Indians Live Today?

Most California Indians now live in much the same way as their non-Indian neighbors. They work similar jobs, wear similar clothes, and live in similar houses.

Preserving native ways

Many California Indians still have strong ties to their **tribes**. That is especially true of Indians who live on **reservations**. There are about 100 reservations in California. They are generally run by tribal councils elected by tribe members. Tribal councils work hard to help their people. They also try to **preserve** the tribe's history. Several reservations operate their own museums.

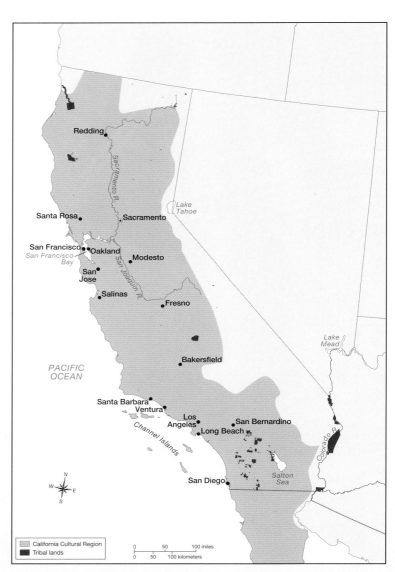

▲ The parts of the map in red show where Indian reservations are located in modern-day California.

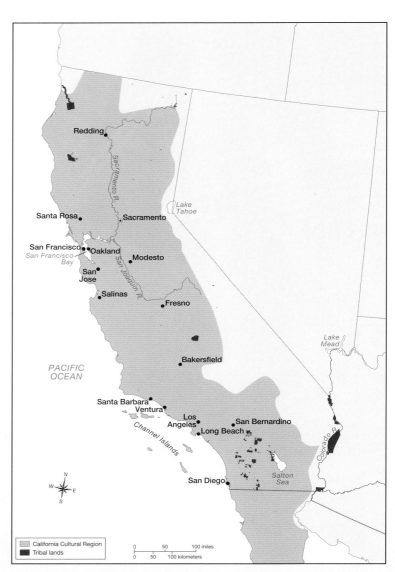
(Map labels: Redding, Sacramento, Lake Tahoe, Santa Rosa, San Francisco, San Francisco Bay, Oakland, Modesto, San Jose, Salinas, Fresno, Bakersfield, Santa Barbara, Ventura, Los Angeles, Long Beach, San Bernardino, San Diego, Salton Sea, Lake Mead, PACIFIC OCEAN, Channel Islands, Sacramento R., San Joaquin R., Colorado R.)

California Cultural Region
Tribal lands

0   50   100 miles
0   50   100 kilometers

For instance, the Hoopa Valley Reservation in northern California is home to a museum in which visitors can learn all about the Hupa people.

California Indian organizations

Other organizations are also working to protect California's Indian **heritage**. The California Indian Basketweavers Association brings together Indians who weave baskets using the methods of their **ancestors**. Members want to educate others about **traditional** basket making and to pass on their skills. The California Indian Storytellers Association works to preserve the stories long told by the California Indians. It hosts events where both Indians and non-Indians can hear these tales from talented **native** storytellers. The California Indian Education Association is devoted to making sure that Indian history is taught accurately in California schools.

▲ By sharing their knowledge with their children and grandchildren, California Indian **elders** help keep their tribes' traditions alive.

Celebrating Indian culture

California Indians also celebrate their **culture** at festivals. At these gatherings, Indian people get a chance to visit with family and friends. They also listen to traditional music and eat traditional foods. Many events feature **ceremonies** and dancing. In central California, some tribes also hold what they call **Big Times**. These fall gatherings mark the beginning of the acorn harvest season. Participants enjoy tasty dishes made from acorns, just as their ancestors did long ago.

On the fourth Friday of September, all of California remembers its Indian heritage. That day is a state holiday called California Native American Day. Schoolchildren from across California celebrate the holiday. Many board buses bound for California State University in San Bernardino to attend the day's biggest event. There, California Indians share their stories, art, music, dances, and food with young people, both Indian and non-Indian. These students all learn a valuable lesson about the important role of Indians not only in California's past, but also in its present and future.

▲ At cultural festivals, California Indians dress in colorful ceremonial clothing to perform their peoples' traditional dances.

◄ In this painting by Harry Fonseca, the character Coyote wears a black leather jacket, blue jeans, and the traditional headdress of some American Indian groups.

BIOGRAPHY

Harry Fonseca

Harry Fonseca (1946–2006) was a very successful American Indian artist. He was a member of the Maidu tribe of northern California. Fonseca was particularly known for his paintings of Coyote, a favorite character in the Maidu's traditional stories. These paintings often featured a modern twist. For example, one shows Coyote in a leather jacket. In another, he is eating cotton candy.

Timeline

about 10,000 BCE	Humans first cross the land bridge into North America
about 8,000 BCE	Humans probably begin living in the California culture area.
1543 CE	Juan Rodríguez Cabrillo leads a Spanish exploration of the California coast.
1579	Sir Francis Drake encounters Indians in northern California.
1769	The Spanish begin building **missions** in California.
1785	The Indians at San Gabriel mission rebel against Spanish rule.
1812	Russians establish a trading post in northern California.
1834	Mexico abandons the Spanish missions and frees the California Indians living there.
1848	Gold is discovered in California.
1850	California becomes an American state.
1952	The United States adopts the relocation policy, which brings large numbers of Indians from other states to California cities.
1968	The American Indian Movement (AIM) organizes protests against the unfair treatment of American Indians and calls on the government to keep its promises to the people.

1969–1970	Indians from across the country come to California to participate in the Alcatraz Island protest.
1990	Congress passes the Native American Language Act, "to **preserve**, protect, and promote the rights and freedoms of all Native Americans to use, practice and develop Native American languages."
1990	President George H.W. Bush proclaims the first National American Indian Heritage Month.
1992	The California Indian Basketweavers Association is established.
1998	California Native American Day becomes a state holiday in California.
2000	The U.S. Census estimates the American Indian population in California to be about 330,000.
2004	The National Museum of the American Indian is established on the national mall in Washington, D.C.
2010	The Smithsonian Institution returns more than 200 artifacts to the Yurok tribe.

Glossary

affiliation membership in a group or organization

ancestor person's relative who lived a long time ago

annual yearly

anthropologist person who studies the way a group of people lived long ago

Big Time contemporary celebration by California Indians of the annual acorn harvest

California Gold Rush event in which people from around the world went to California to seek gold

ceremony religious event or observance

convert persuade another person to adopt a different religion

culture shared ways of life and beliefs of a people

culture area region of North America in which Indians traditionally had a similar way of life

descendant person's relative who lives a long time after he or she

elder older person

expedition trip taken for a specific purpose

gamble to bet on a game

game wild animals hunted for food

heritage cultural traditions that have been passed down from generation to generation

homeland original territory of a group of people

lacrosse team sport in which players try to throw a ball into a goal using a long stick that has a pouch

marsh low-lying area that often floods

measles disease that causes a fever and a red rash

miner person who digs minerals, such as gold or coal, out of the ground

mission building or buildings constructed by a religious group hoping to convince local people to convert to the group's religion

moccasin slipper-like shoe made of soft leather

mussel water creature that has a hard black shell

native person born in a specific place

natural resources land, water, forest, and other features of nature that humans can use

oasis area in a desert where there is water and plants

preserve to keep something from changing

ramada raised platform that provides shade

reed type of tall grass that grows in the water or in watery grass

reservation area of land put aside for the use of a group of American Indians

resort to turn to

scallop water creature that has a fan-shaped shell

smallpox disease that causes a fever and blisters on the skin

spring place where water from an underground source springs to the surface

tomol canoe made of planks of wood used by the Chumash tribe

traditional something, such as food, clothing, or houses, from the time before Indians had contact with non-Indians

tribe group of American Indians who share a culture

tule plant that grows wild in marshy areas of California

weir trap used to catch fish

Find Out More

Books

Feinstein, Stephen. *California Native Peoples*. Chicago: Heinemann-Raintree, 2009.

Gendell, Megan. *The Spanish Missions of California*. New York: Children's Press, 2010.

Sonneborn, Liz. *The Chumash*. Minneapolis, Minn.: Lerner Publications, 2007.

Williams, Jack S. *The Miwok of California*. New York: PowerKids, 2004.

Websites

California Indian Basketweavers Association
www.ciba.org
The California Indian Basketweavers Association site provides information about this organization and its prominent members.

California Indian Food and Culture
http://hearstmuseum.berkeley.edu/outreach/pdfs/teaching_kit.pdf
This online booklet describes the many foods traditionally enjoyed by the Indians of California.

California Indian Heritage Center
www.parks.ca.gov/default.asp?page_id=22628
The California Indian Heritage Center provides information about California Indian basketry and languages.

California Native American Day
www.nativeamericanday.com
This site describes California's annual Native American Day and features video highlights from recent celebrations.

DVDs

The Gold Rush. DVD. Directed by Randall MacLowry. Paramount Home Video, 2006.

The Last of His Tribe. DVD. Directed by Harry Hook. New York, NY: HBO Home Video, 2004.

Places to visit

California Indian Museum and Cultural Center
5250 Aero Drive
Santa Rosa, CA
www.cimcc.org/

California State Indian Museum
2618 K Street
Sacramento, CA
www.parks.ca.gov/default.asp?page_id=486

Further research

From this book, you discovered information on California Indians. But there is plenty more to learn. Below are some topics you might enjoy researching.

California Indian baskets: Many art or natural history museums have baskets made by California Indians in their collections. Next time you visit a museum, ask the staff if they have any on display.

Traditional foods of California Indians: Use the online booklet available at http://hearstmuseum.berkeley.edu/outreach/pdfs/teaching_kit.pdf to make a list of traditional California Indian foods. Put a check by any of the foods you have eaten. Whenever you get a chance, try a new food on the list so you can check it off.

Index